Food Recall and Withdrawal Log

by Joshua R. Embry | www.embryinc.com

Food recalls or withdrawals can differ in type and response. While recalls usually represent a real or perceived threat to public health, withdrawals may occur when there is a quality issue or the possibility of contamination. Regardless of which type occurs, it is in your organization's best interest to log how you or your team appropriately dealt with the issue. A log ensures proper processing and handling of a recall that can also provide a written record of the steps your organization has taken to limit the spread or use of affected product. The safety of your staff and guests should remain a high priority within your facility.

One log should be onsite at <u>each</u> operating facility.

Facility Name:_____

Facility Address:_____

Date Notified:	Notification Method: (Email, Phone, etc.)	Product Description:	Product Identifier or Product Code:	Quantity on Hand: (incl. cases or eaches)

Was illness reported at your facility?	
Resolution: (Product destroyed, returned, etc.)	
Name Person Handling Recall/Withdrawal: (at your facility)	

Date Notified:	Notification Method: (Email, Phone, etc.)	Product Description:	Product Identifier or Product Code:	Quantity on Hand: (incl. cases or eaches)

Was illness reported at your facility?	
Resolution: (Product destroyed, returned, etc.)	
Name Person Handling Recall/Withdrawal: (at your facility)	

Date Notified:	Notification Method: (Email, Phone, etc.)	Product Description:	Product Identifier or Product Code:	Quantity on Hand: (incl. cases or eaches)

Was illness reported at your facility?	
Resolution: (Product destroyed, returned, etc.)	
Name Person Handling Recall/Withdrawal: (at your facility)	

Date Notified:	Notification Method: (Email, Phone, etc.)	Product Description:	Product Identifier or Product Code:	Quantity on Hand: (incl. cases or eaches)
Was illness reported at your facility?				
Resolution: (Product destroyed, returned, etc.)				
Name Person Handling Recall/Withdrawal: (at your facility)				

Date Notified:	Notification Method: (Email, Phone, etc.)	Product Description:	Product Identifier or Product Code:	Quantity on Hand: (incl. cases or eaches)
Was illness reported at your facility?				
Resolution: (Product destroyed, returned, etc.)				
Name Person Handling Recall/Withdrawal: (at your facility)				

Date Notified:	Notification Method: (Email, Phone, etc.)	Product Description:	Product Identifier or Product Code:	Quantity on Hand: (incl. cases or eaches)
Was illness reported at your facility?				
Resolution: (Product destroyed, returned, etc.)				
Name Person Handling Recall/Withdrawal: (at your facility)				

Date Notified:	Notification Method: (Email, Phone, etc.)	Product Description:	Product Identifier or Product Code:	Quantity on Hand: (incl. cases or eaches)

Was illness reported at your facility?	
Resolution: (Product destroyed, returned, etc.)	
Name Person Handling Recall/Withdrawal: (at your facility)	

Date Notified:	Notification Method: (Email, Phone, etc.)	Product Description:	Product Identifier or Product Code:	Quantity on Hand: (incl. cases or eaches)

Was illness reported at your facility?	
Resolution: (Product destroyed, returned, etc.)	
Name Person Handling Recall/Withdrawal: (at your facility)	

Date Notified:	Notification Method: (Email, Phone, etc.)	Product Description:	Product Identifier or Product Code:	Quantity on Hand: (incl. cases or eaches)

Was illness reported at your facility?	
Resolution: (Product destroyed, returned, etc.)	
Name Person Handling Recall/Withdrawal: (at your facility)	

Date Notified:	Notification Method: (Email, Phone, etc.)	Product Description:	Product Identifier or Product Code:	Quantity on Hand: (incl. cases or eaches)

Was illness reported at your facility?	
Resolution: (Product destroyed, returned, etc.)	
Name Person Handling Recall/Withdrawal: (at your facility)	

Date Notified:	Notification Method: (Email, Phone, etc.)	Product Description:	Product Identifier or Product Code:	Quantity on Hand: (incl. cases or eaches)

Was illness reported at your facility?	
Resolution: (Product destroyed, returned, etc.)	
Name Person Handling Recall/Withdrawal: (at your facility)	

Date Notified:	Notification Method: (Email, Phone, etc.)	Product Description:	Product Identifier or Product Code:	Quantity on Hand: (incl. cases or eaches)

Was illness reported at your facility?	
Resolution: (Product destroyed, returned, etc.)	
Name Person Handling Recall/Withdrawal: (at your facility)	

Date Notified:	Notification Method: (Email, Phone, etc.)	Product Description:	Product Identifier or Product Code:	Quantity on Hand: (incl. cases or eaches)

Was illness reported at your facility?	
Resolution: (Product destroyed, returned, etc.)	
Name Person Handling Recall/Withdrawal: (at your facility)	

Date Notified:	Notification Method: (Email, Phone, etc.)	Product Description:	Product Identifier or Product Code:	Quantity on Hand: (incl. cases or eaches)

Was illness reported at your facility?	
Resolution: (Product destroyed, returned, etc.)	
Name Person Handling Recall/Withdrawal: (at your facility)	

Date Notified:	Notification Method: (Email, Phone, etc.)	Product Description:	Product Identifier or Product Code:	Quantity on Hand: (incl. cases or eaches)

Was illness reported at your facility?	
Resolution: (Product destroyed, returned, etc.)	
Name Person Handling Recall/Withdrawal: (at your facility)	

Date Notified:	Notification Method: (Email, Phone, etc.)	Product Description:	Product Identifier or Product Code:	Quantity on Hand: (incl. cases or eaches)
Was illness reported at your facility?				
Resolution: (Product destroyed, returned, etc.)				
Name Person Handling Recall/Withdrawal: (at your facility)				

Date Notified:	Notification Method: (Email, Phone, etc.)	Product Description:	Product Identifier or Product Code:	Quantity on Hand: (incl. cases or eaches)
Was illness reported at your facility?				
Resolution: (Product destroyed, returned, etc.)				
Name Person Handling Recall/Withdrawal: (at your facility)				

Date Notified:	Notification Method: (Email, Phone, etc.)	Product Description:	Product Identifier or Product Code:	Quantity on Hand: (incl. cases or eaches)
Was illness reported at your facility?				
Resolution: (Product destroyed, returned, etc.)				
Name Person Handling Recall/Withdrawal: (at your facility)				

Date Notified:	Notification Method: (Email, Phone, etc.)	Product Description:	Product Identifier or Product Code:	Quantity on Hand: (incl. cases or eaches)

Was illness reported at your facility?	
Resolution: (Product destroyed, returned, etc.)	
Name Person Handling Recall/Withdrawal: (at your facility)	

Date Notified:	Notification Method: (Email, Phone, etc.)	Product Description:	Product Identifier or Product Code:	Quantity on Hand: (incl. cases or eaches)

Was illness reported at your facility?	
Resolution: (Product destroyed, returned, etc.)	
Name Person Handling Recall/Withdrawal: (at your facility)	

Date Notified:	Notification Method: (Email, Phone, etc.)	Product Description:	Product Identifier or Product Code:	Quantity on Hand: (incl. cases or eaches)

Was illness reported at your facility?	
Resolution: (Product destroyed, returned, etc.)	
Name Person Handling Recall/Withdrawal: (at your facility)	

Date Notified:	Notification Method: (Email, Phone, etc.)	Product Description:	Product Identifier or Product Code:	Quantity on Hand: (incl. cases or eaches)

Was illness reported at your facility?	
Resolution: (Product destroyed, returned, etc.)	
Name Person Handling Recall/Withdrawal: (at your facility)	

Date Notified:	Notification Method: (Email, Phone, etc.)	Product Description:	Product Identifier or Product Code:	Quantity on Hand: (incl. cases or eaches)

Was illness reported at your facility?	
Resolution: (Product destroyed, returned, etc.)	
Name Person Handling Recall/Withdrawal: (at your facility)	

Date Notified:	Notification Method: (Email, Phone, etc.)	Product Description:	Product Identifier or Product Code:	Quantity on Hand: (incl. cases or eaches)

Was illness reported at your facility?	
Resolution: (Product destroyed, returned, etc.)	
Name Person Handling Recall/Withdrawal: (at your facility)	

Date Notified:	Notification Method: (Email, Phone, etc.)	Product Description:	Product Identifier or Product Code:	Quantity on Hand: (incl. cases or eaches)

Was illness reported at your facility?	
Resolution: (Product destroyed, returned, etc.)	
Name Person Handling Recall/Withdrawal: (at your facility)	

Date Notified:	Notification Method: (Email, Phone, etc.)	Product Description:	Product Identifier or Product Code:	Quantity on Hand: (incl. cases or eaches)

Was illness reported at your facility?	
Resolution: (Product destroyed, returned, etc.)	
Name Person Handling Recall/Withdrawal: (at your facility)	

Date Notified:	Notification Method: (Email, Phone, etc.)	Product Description:	Product Identifier or Product Code:	Quantity on Hand: (incl. cases or eaches)

Was illness reported at your facility?	
Resolution: (Product destroyed, returned, etc.)	
Name Person Handling Recall/Withdrawal: (at your facility)	

Date Notified:	Notification Method: (Email, Phone, etc.)	Product Description:	Product Identifier or Product Code:	Quantity on Hand: (incl. cases or eaches)

Was illness reported at your facility?	
Resolution: (Product destroyed, returned, etc.)	
Name Person Handling Recall/Withdrawal: (at your facility)	

Date Notified:	Notification Method: (Email, Phone, etc.)	Product Description:	Product Identifier or Product Code:	Quantity on Hand: (incl. cases or eaches)

Was illness reported at your facility?	
Resolution: (Product destroyed, returned, etc.)	
Name Person Handling Recall/Withdrawal: (at your facility)	

Date Notified:	Notification Method: (Email, Phone, etc.)	Product Description:	Product Identifier or Product Code:	Quantity on Hand: (incl. cases or eaches)

Was illness reported at your facility?	
Resolution: (Product destroyed, returned, etc.)	
Name Person Handling Recall/Withdrawal: (at your facility)	

Date Notified:	Notification Method: (Email, Phone, etc.)	Product Description:	Product Identifier or Product Code:	Quantity on Hand: (incl. cases or eaches)
Was illness reported at your facility?				
Resolution: (Product destroyed, returned, etc.)				
Name Person Handling Recall/Withdrawal: (at your facility)				

Date Notified:	Notification Method: (Email, Phone, etc.)	Product Description:	Product Identifier or Product Code:	Quantity on Hand: (incl. cases or eaches)
Was illness reported at your facility?				
Resolution: (Product destroyed, returned, etc.)				
Name Person Handling Recall/Withdrawal: (at your facility)				

Date Notified:	Notification Method: (Email, Phone, etc.)	Product Description:	Product Identifier or Product Code:	Quantity on Hand: (incl. cases or eaches)
Was illness reported at your facility?				
Resolution: (Product destroyed, returned, etc.)				
Name Person Handling Recall/Withdrawal: (at your facility)				

Date Notified:	Notification Method: (Email, Phone, etc.)	Product Description:	Product Identifier or Product Code:	Quantity on Hand: (incl. cases or eaches)

Was illness reported at your facility?	
Resolution: (Product destroyed, returned, etc.)	
Name Person Handling Recall/Withdrawal: (at your facility)	

Date Notified:	Notification Method: (Email, Phone, etc.)	Product Description:	Product Identifier or Product Code:	Quantity on Hand: (incl. cases or eaches)

Was illness reported at your facility?	
Resolution: (Product destroyed, returned, etc.)	
Name Person Handling Recall/Withdrawal: (at your facility)	

Date Notified:	Notification Method: (Email, Phone, etc.)	Product Description:	Product Identifier or Product Code:	Quantity on Hand: (incl. cases or eaches)

Was illness reported at your facility?	
Resolution: (Product destroyed, returned, etc.)	
Name Person Handling Recall/Withdrawal: (at your facility)	

Date Notified:	Notification Method: (Email, Phone, etc.)	Product Description:	Product Identifier or Product Code:	Quantity on Hand: (incl. cases or eaches)

Was illness reported at your facility?	
Resolution: (Product destroyed, returned, etc.)	
Name Person Handling Recall/Withdrawal: (at your facility)	

Date Notified:	Notification Method: (Email, Phone, etc.)	Product Description:	Product Identifier or Product Code:	Quantity on Hand: (incl. cases or eaches)

Was illness reported at your facility?	
Resolution: (Product destroyed, returned, etc.)	
Name Person Handling Recall/Withdrawal: (at your facility)	

Date Notified:	Notification Method: (Email, Phone, etc.)	Product Description:	Product Identifier or Product Code:	Quantity on Hand: (incl. cases or eaches)

Was illness reported at your facility?	
Resolution: (Product destroyed, returned, etc.)	
Name Person Handling Recall/Withdrawal: (at your facility)	

Date Notified:	Notification Method: (Email, Phone, etc.)	Product Description:	Product Identifier or Product Code:	Quantity on Hand: (incl. cases or eaches)

Was illness reported at your facility?	
Resolution: (Product destroyed, returned, etc.)	
Name Person Handling Recall/Withdrawal: (at your facility)	

Date Notified:	Notification Method: (Email, Phone, etc.)	Product Description:	Product Identifier or Product Code:	Quantity on Hand: (incl. cases or eaches)

Was illness reported at your facility?	
Resolution: (Product destroyed, returned, etc.)	
Name Person Handling Recall/Withdrawal: (at your facility)	

Date Notified:	Notification Method: (Email, Phone, etc.)	Product Description:	Product Identifier or Product Code:	Quantity on Hand: (incl. cases or eaches)

Was illness reported at your facility?	
Resolution: (Product destroyed, returned, etc.)	
Name Person Handling Recall/Withdrawal: (at your facility)	

Date Notified:	Notification Method: (Email, Phone, etc.)	Product Description:	Product Identifier or Product Code:	Quantity on Hand: (incl. cases or eaches)

Was illness reported at your facility?	
Resolution: (Product destroyed, returned, etc.)	
Name Person Handling Recall/Withdrawal: (at your facility)	

Date Notified:	Notification Method: (Email, Phone, etc.)	Product Description:	Product Identifier or Product Code:	Quantity on Hand: (incl. cases or eaches)

Was illness reported at your facility?	
Resolution: (Product destroyed, returned, etc.)	
Name Person Handling Recall/Withdrawal: (at your facility)	

Date Notified:	Notification Method: (Email, Phone, etc.)	Product Description:	Product Identifier or Product Code:	Quantity on Hand: (incl. cases or eaches)

Was illness reported at your facility?	
Resolution: (Product destroyed, returned, etc.)	
Name Person Handling Recall/Withdrawal: (at your facility)	

Date Notified:	Notification Method: (Email, Phone, etc.)	Product Description:	Product Identifier or Product Code:	Quantity on Hand: (incl. cases or eaches)

Was illness reported at your facility?	
Resolution: (Product destroyed, returned, etc.)	
Name Person Handling Recall/Withdrawal: (at your facility)	

Date Notified:	Notification Method: (Email, Phone, etc.)	Product Description:	Product Identifier or Product Code:	Quantity on Hand: (incl. cases or eaches)

Was illness reported at your facility?	
Resolution: (Product destroyed, returned, etc.)	
Name Person Handling Recall/Withdrawal: (at your facility)	

Date Notified:	Notification Method: (Email, Phone, etc.)	Product Description:	Product Identifier or Product Code:	Quantity on Hand: (incl. cases or eaches)

Was illness reported at your facility?	
Resolution: (Product destroyed, returned, etc.)	
Name Person Handling Recall/Withdrawal: (at your facility)	

Date Notified:	Notification Method: (Email, Phone, etc.)	Product Description:	Product Identifier or Product Code:	Quantity on Hand: (incl. cases or eaches)

Was illness reported at your facility?	
Resolution: (Product destroyed, returned, etc.)	
Name Person Handling Recall/Withdrawal: (at your facility)	

Date Notified:	Notification Method: (Email, Phone, etc.)	Product Description:	Product Identifier or Product Code:	Quantity on Hand: (incl. cases or eaches)

Was illness reported at your facility?	
Resolution: (Product destroyed, returned, etc.)	
Name Person Handling Recall/Withdrawal: (at your facility)	

Date Notified:	Notification Method: (Email, Phone, etc.)	Product Description:	Product Identifier or Product Code:	Quantity on Hand: (incl. cases or eaches)

Was illness reported at your facility?	
Resolution: (Product destroyed, returned, etc.)	
Name Person Handling Recall/Withdrawal: (at your facility)	

Date Notified:	Notification Method: (Email, Phone, etc.)	Product Description:	Product Identifier or Product Code:	Quantity on Hand: (incl. cases or eaches)

Was illness reported at your facility?	
Resolution: (Product destroyed, returned, etc.)	
Name Person Handling Recall/Withdrawal: (at your facility)	

Date Notified:	Notification Method: (Email, Phone, etc.)	Product Description:	Product Identifier or Product Code:	Quantity on Hand: (incl. cases or eaches)

Was illness reported at your facility?	
Resolution: (Product destroyed, returned, etc.)	
Name Person Handling Recall/Withdrawal: (at your facility)	

Date Notified:	Notification Method: (Email, Phone, etc.)	Product Description:	Product Identifier or Product Code:	Quantity on Hand: (incl. cases or eaches)

Was illness reported at your facility?	
Resolution: (Product destroyed, returned, etc.)	
Name Person Handling Recall/Withdrawal: (at your facility)	

Date Notified:	Notification Method: (Email, Phone, etc.)	Product Description:	Product Identifier or Product Code:	Quantity on Hand: (incl. cases or eaches)

Was illness reported at your facility?	
Resolution: (Product destroyed, returned, etc.)	
Name Person Handling Recall/Withdrawal: (at your facility)	

Date Notified:	Notification Method: (Email, Phone, etc.)	Product Description:	Product Identifier or Product Code:	Quantity on Hand: (incl. cases or eaches)

Was illness reported at your facility?	
Resolution: (Product destroyed, returned, etc.)	
Name Person Handling Recall/Withdrawal: (at your facility)	

Date Notified:	Notification Method: (Email, Phone, etc.)	Product Description:	Product Identifier or Product Code:	Quantity on Hand: (incl. cases or eaches)

Was illness reported at your facility?	
Resolution: (Product destroyed, returned, etc.)	
Name Person Handling Recall/Withdrawal: (at your facility)	

Date Notified:	Notification Method: (Email, Phone, etc.)	Product Description:	Product Identifier or Product Code:	Quantity on Hand: (incl. cases or eaches)
Was illness reported at your facility?				
Resolution: (Product destroyed, returned, etc.)				
Name Person Handling Recall/Withdrawal: (at your facility)				

Date Notified:	Notification Method: (Email, Phone, etc.)	Product Description:	Product Identifier or Product Code:	Quantity on Hand: (incl. cases or eaches)
Was illness reported at your facility?				
Resolution: (Product destroyed, returned, etc.)				
Name Person Handling Recall/Withdrawal: (at your facility)				

Date Notified:	Notification Method: (Email, Phone, etc.)	Product Description:	Product Identifier or Product Code:	Quantity on Hand: (incl. cases or eaches)
Was illness reported at your facility?				
Resolution: (Product destroyed, returned, etc.)				
Name Person Handling Recall/Withdrawal: (at your facility)				

Date Notified:	Notification Method: (Email, Phone, etc.)	Product Description:	Product Identifier or Product Code:	Quantity on Hand: (incl. cases or eaches)
Was illness reported at your facility?				
Resolution: (Product destroyed, returned, etc.)				
Name Person Handling Recall/Withdrawal: (at your facility)				

Date Notified:	Notification Method: (Email, Phone, etc.)	Product Description:	Product Identifier or Product Code:	Quantity on Hand: (incl. cases or eaches)
Was illness reported at your facility?				
Resolution: (Product destroyed, returned, etc.)				
Name Person Handling Recall/Withdrawal: (at your facility)				

Date Notified:	Notification Method: (Email, Phone, etc.)	Product Description:	Product Identifier or Product Code:	Quantity on Hand: (incl. cases or eaches)
Was illness reported at your facility?				
Resolution: (Product destroyed, returned, etc.)				
Name Person Handling Recall/Withdrawal: (at your facility)				

Date Notified:	Notification Method: (Email, Phone, etc.)	Product Description:	Product Identifier or Product Code:	Quantity on Hand: (incl. cases or eaches)
Was illness reported at your facility?				
Resolution: (Product destroyed, returned, etc.)				
Name Person Handling Recall/Withdrawal: (at your facility)				

Date Notified:	Notification Method: (Email, Phone, etc.)	Product Description:	Product Identifier or Product Code:	Quantity on Hand: (incl. cases or eaches)
Was illness reported at your facility?				
Resolution: (Product destroyed, returned, etc.)				
Name Person Handling Recall/Withdrawal: (at your facility)				

Date Notified:	Notification Method: (Email, Phone, etc.)	Product Description:	Product Identifier or Product Code:	Quantity on Hand: (incl. cases or eaches)
Was illness reported at your facility?				
Resolution: (Product destroyed, returned, etc.)				
Name Person Handling Recall/Withdrawal: (at your facility)				

Date Notified:	Notification Method: (Email, Phone, etc.)	Product Description:	Product Identifier or Product Code:	Quantity on Hand: (incl. cases or eaches)

Was illness reported at your facility?	
Resolution: (Product destroyed, returned, etc.)	
Name Person Handling Recall/Withdrawal: (at your facility)	

Date Notified:	Notification Method: (Email, Phone, etc.)	Product Description:	Product Identifier or Product Code:	Quantity on Hand: (incl. cases or eaches)

Was illness reported at your facility?	
Resolution: (Product destroyed, returned, etc.)	
Name Person Handling Recall/Withdrawal: (at your facility)	

Date Notified:	Notification Method: (Email, Phone, etc.)	Product Description:	Product Identifier or Product Code:	Quantity on Hand: (incl. cases or eaches)

Was illness reported at your facility?	
Resolution: (Product destroyed, returned, etc.)	
Name Person Handling Recall/Withdrawal: (at your facility)	

Date Notified:	Notification Method: (Email, Phone, etc.)	Product Description:	Product Identifier or Product Code:	Quantity on Hand: (incl. cases or eaches)

Was illness reported at your facility?	
Resolution: (Product destroyed, returned, etc.)	
Name Person Handling Recall/Withdrawal: (at your facility)	

Date Notified:	Notification Method: (Email, Phone, etc.)	Product Description:	Product Identifier or Product Code:	Quantity on Hand: (incl. cases or eaches)

Was illness reported at your facility?	
Resolution: (Product destroyed, returned, etc.)	
Name Person Handling Recall/Withdrawal: (at your facility)	

Date Notified:	Notification Method: (Email, Phone, etc.)	Product Description:	Product Identifier or Product Code:	Quantity on Hand: (incl. cases or eaches)

Was illness reported at your facility?	
Resolution: (Product destroyed, returned, etc.)	
Name Person Handling Recall/Withdrawal: (at your facility)	

Date Notified:	Notification Method: (Email, Phone, etc.)	Product Description:	Product Identifier or Product Code:	Quantity on Hand: (incl. cases or eaches)

Was illness reported at your facility?	
Resolution: (Product destroyed, returned, etc.)	
Name Person Handling Recall/Withdrawal: (at your facility)	

Date Notified:	Notification Method: (Email, Phone, etc.)	Product Description:	Product Identifier or Product Code:	Quantity on Hand: (incl. cases or eaches)

Was illness reported at your facility?	
Resolution: (Product destroyed, returned, etc.)	
Name Person Handling Recall/Withdrawal: (at your facility)	

Date Notified:	Notification Method: (Email, Phone, etc.)	Product Description:	Product Identifier or Product Code:	Quantity on Hand: (incl. cases or eaches)

Was illness reported at your facility?	
Resolution: (Product destroyed, returned, etc.)	
Name Person Handling Recall/Withdrawal: (at your facility)	

Date Notified:	Notification Method: (Email, Phone, etc.)	Product Description:	Product Identifier or Product Code:	Quantity on Hand: (incl. cases or eaches)
Was illness reported at your facility?				
Resolution: (Product destroyed, returned, etc.)				
Name Person Handling Recall/Withdrawal: (at your facility)				

Date Notified:	Notification Method: (Email, Phone, etc.)	Product Description:	Product Identifier or Product Code:	Quantity on Hand: (incl. cases or eaches)
Was illness reported at your facility?				
Resolution: (Product destroyed, returned, etc.)				
Name Person Handling Recall/Withdrawal: (at your facility)				

Date Notified:	Notification Method: (Email, Phone, etc.)	Product Description:	Product Identifier or Product Code:	Quantity on Hand: (incl. cases or eaches)
Was illness reported at your facility?				
Resolution: (Product destroyed, returned, etc.)				
Name Person Handling Recall/Withdrawal: (at your facility)				

Date Notified:	Notification Method: (Email, Phone, etc.)	Product Description:	Product Identifier or Product Code:	Quantity on Hand: (incl. cases or eaches)

Was illness reported at your facility?	
Resolution: (Product destroyed, returned, etc.)	
Name Person Handling Recall/Withdrawal: (at your facility)	

Date Notified:	Notification Method: (Email, Phone, etc.)	Product Description:	Product Identifier or Product Code:	Quantity on Hand: (incl. cases or eaches)

Was illness reported at your facility?	
Resolution: (Product destroyed, returned, etc.)	
Name Person Handling Recall/Withdrawal: (at your facility)	

Date Notified:	Notification Method: (Email, Phone, etc.)	Product Description:	Product Identifier or Product Code:	Quantity on Hand: (incl. cases or eaches)

Was illness reported at your facility?	
Resolution: (Product destroyed, returned, etc.)	
Name Person Handling Recall/Withdrawal: (at your facility)	

Date Notified:	Notification Method: (Email, Phone, etc.)	Product Description:	Product Identifier or Product Code:	Quantity on Hand: (incl. cases or eaches)
Was illness reported at your facility?				
Resolution: (Product destroyed, returned, etc.)				
Name Person Handling Recall/Withdrawal: (at your facility)				

Date Notified:	Notification Method: (Email, Phone, etc.)	Product Description:	Product Identifier or Product Code:	Quantity on Hand: (incl. cases or eaches)
Was illness reported at your facility?				
Resolution: (Product destroyed, returned, etc.)				
Name Person Handling Recall/Withdrawal: (at your facility)				

Date Notified:	Notification Method: (Email, Phone, etc.)	Product Description:	Product Identifier or Product Code:	Quantity on Hand: (incl. cases or eaches)
Was illness reported at your facility?				
Resolution: (Product destroyed, returned, etc.)				
Name Person Handling Recall/Withdrawal: (at your facility)				

Date Notified:	Notification Method: (Email, Phone, etc.)	Product Description:	Product Identifier or Product Code:	Quantity on Hand: (incl. cases or eaches)

Was illness reported at your facility?	
Resolution: (Product destroyed, returned, etc.)	
Name Person Handling Recall/Withdrawal: (at your facility)	

Date Notified:	Notification Method: (Email, Phone, etc.)	Product Description:	Product Identifier or Product Code:	Quantity on Hand: (incl. cases or eaches)

Was illness reported at your facility?	
Resolution: (Product destroyed, returned, etc.)	
Name Person Handling Recall/Withdrawal: (at your facility)	

Date Notified:	Notification Method: (Email, Phone, etc.)	Product Description:	Product Identifier or Product Code:	Quantity on Hand: (incl. cases or eaches)

Was illness reported at your facility?	
Resolution: (Product destroyed, returned, etc.)	
Name Person Handling Recall/Withdrawal: (at your facility)	

Date Notified:	Notification Method: (Email, Phone, etc.)	Product Description:	Product Identifier or Product Code:	Quantity on Hand: (incl. cases or eaches)
Was illness reported at your facility?				
Resolution: (Product destroyed, returned, etc.)				
Name Person Handling Recall/Withdrawal: (at your facility)				

Date Notified:	Notification Method: (Email, Phone, etc.)	Product Description:	Product Identifier or Product Code:	Quantity on Hand: (incl. cases or eaches)
Was illness reported at your facility?				
Resolution: (Product destroyed, returned, etc.)				
Name Person Handling Recall/Withdrawal: (at your facility)				

Date Notified:	Notification Method: (Email, Phone, etc.)	Product Description:	Product Identifier or Product Code:	Quantity on Hand: (incl. cases or eaches)
Was illness reported at your facility?				
Resolution: (Product destroyed, returned, etc.)				
Name Person Handling Recall/Withdrawal: (at your facility)				

Date Notified:	Notification Method: (Email, Phone, etc.)	Product Description:	Product Identifier or Product Code:	Quantity on Hand: (incl. cases or eaches)

Was illness reported at your facility?	
Resolution: (Product destroyed, returned, etc.)	
Name Person Handling Recall/Withdrawal: (at your facility)	

Date Notified:	Notification Method: (Email, Phone, etc.)	Product Description:	Product Identifier or Product Code:	Quantity on Hand: (incl. cases or eaches)

Was illness reported at your facility?	
Resolution: (Product destroyed, returned, etc.)	
Name Person Handling Recall/Withdrawal: (at your facility)	

Date Notified:	Notification Method: (Email, Phone, etc.)	Product Description:	Product Identifier or Product Code:	Quantity on Hand: (incl. cases or eaches)

Was illness reported at your facility?	
Resolution: (Product destroyed, returned, etc.)	
Name Person Handling Recall/Withdrawal: (at your facility)	

Date Notified:	Notification Method: (Email, Phone, etc.)	Product Description:	Product Identifier or Product Code:	Quantity on Hand: (incl. cases or eaches)

Was illness reported at your facility?	
Resolution: (Product destroyed, returned, etc.)	
Name Person Handling Recall/Withdrawal: (at your facility)	

Date Notified:	Notification Method: (Email, Phone, etc.)	Product Description:	Product Identifier or Product Code:	Quantity on Hand: (incl. cases or eaches)

Was illness reported at your facility?	
Resolution: (Product destroyed, returned, etc.)	
Name Person Handling Recall/Withdrawal: (at your facility)	

Date Notified:	Notification Method: (Email, Phone, etc.)	Product Description:	Product Identifier or Product Code:	Quantity on Hand: (incl. cases or eaches)

Was illness reported at your facility?	
Resolution: (Product destroyed, returned, etc.)	
Name Person Handling Recall/Withdrawal: (at your facility)	

Date Notified:	Notification Method: (Email, Phone, etc.)	Product Description:	Product Identifier or Product Code:	Quantity on Hand: (incl. cases or eaches)

Was illness reported at your facility?	
Resolution: (Product destroyed, returned, etc.)	
Name Person Handling Recall/Withdrawal: (at your facility)	

Date Notified:	Notification Method: (Email, Phone, etc.)	Product Description:	Product Identifier or Product Code:	Quantity on Hand: (incl. cases or eaches)

Was illness reported at your facility?	
Resolution: (Product destroyed, returned, etc.)	
Name Person Handling Recall/Withdrawal: (at your facility)	

Date Notified:	Notification Method: (Email, Phone, etc.)	Product Description:	Product Identifier or Product Code:	Quantity on Hand: (incl. cases or eaches)

Was illness reported at your facility?	
Resolution: (Product destroyed, returned, etc.)	
Name Person Handling Recall/Withdrawal: (at your facility)	

Date Notified:	Notification Method: (Email, Phone, etc.)	Product Description:	Product Identifier or Product Code:	Quantity on Hand: (incl. cases or eaches)
Was illness reported at your facility?				
Resolution: (Product destroyed, returned, etc.)				
Name Person Handling Recall/Withdrawal: (at your facility)				

Date Notified:	Notification Method: (Email, Phone, etc.)	Product Description:	Product Identifier or Product Code:	Quantity on Hand: (incl. cases or eaches)
Was illness reported at your facility?				
Resolution: (Product destroyed, returned, etc.)				
Name Person Handling Recall/Withdrawal: (at your facility)				

Date Notified:	Notification Method: (Email, Phone, etc.)	Product Description:	Product Identifier or Product Code:	Quantity on Hand: (incl. cases or eaches)
Was illness reported at your facility?				
Resolution: (Product destroyed, returned, etc.)				
Name Person Handling Recall/Withdrawal: (at your facility)				

Date Notified:	Notification Method: (Email, Phone, etc.)	Product Description:	Product Identifier or Product Code:	Quantity on Hand: (incl. cases or eaches)
Was illness reported at your facility?				
Resolution: (Product destroyed, returned, etc.)				
Name Person Handling Recall/Withdrawal: (at your facility)				

Date Notified:	Notification Method: (Email, Phone, etc.)	Product Description:	Product Identifier or Product Code:	Quantity on Hand: (incl. cases or eaches)
Was illness reported at your facility?				
Resolution: (Product destroyed, returned, etc.)				
Name Person Handling Recall/Withdrawal: (at your facility)				

Date Notified:	Notification Method: (Email, Phone, etc.)	Product Description:	Product Identifier or Product Code:	Quantity on Hand: (incl. cases or eaches)
Was illness reported at your facility?				
Resolution: (Product destroyed, returned, etc.)				
Name Person Handling Recall/Withdrawal: (at your facility)				

Date Notified:	Notification Method: (Email, Phone, etc.)	Product Description:	Product Identifier or Product Code:	Quantity on Hand: (incl. cases or eaches)

Was illness reported at your facility?	
Resolution: (Product destroyed, returned, etc.)	
Name Person Handling Recall/Withdrawal: (at your facility)	

Date Notified:	Notification Method: (Email, Phone, etc.)	Product Description:	Product Identifier or Product Code:	Quantity on Hand: (incl. cases or eaches)

Was illness reported at your facility?	
Resolution: (Product destroyed, returned, etc.)	
Name Person Handling Recall/Withdrawal: (at your facility)	

Date Notified:	Notification Method: (Email, Phone, etc.)	Product Description:	Product Identifier or Product Code:	Quantity on Hand: (incl. cases or eaches)

Was illness reported at your facility?	
Resolution: (Product destroyed, returned, etc.)	
Name Person Handling Recall/Withdrawal: (at your facility)	

Date Notified:	Notification Method: (Email, Phone, etc.)	Product Description:	Product Identifier or Product Code:	Quantity on Hand: (incl. cases or eaches)

Was illness reported at your facility?	
Resolution: (Product destroyed, returned, etc.)	
Name Person Handling Recall/Withdrawal: (at your facility)	

Date Notified:	Notification Method: (Email, Phone, etc.)	Product Description:	Product Identifier or Product Code:	Quantity on Hand: (incl. cases or eaches)

Was illness reported at your facility?	
Resolution: (Product destroyed, returned, etc.)	
Name Person Handling Recall/Withdrawal: (at your facility)	

Date Notified:	Notification Method: (Email, Phone, etc.)	Product Description:	Product Identifier or Product Code:	Quantity on Hand: (incl. cases or eaches)

Was illness reported at your facility?	
Resolution: (Product destroyed, returned, etc.)	
Name Person Handling Recall/Withdrawal: (at your facility)	

Date Notified:	Notification Method: (Email, Phone, etc.)	Product Description:	Product Identifier or Product Code:	Quantity on Hand: (incl. cases or eaches)

Was illness reported at your facility?	
Resolution: (Product destroyed, returned, etc.)	
Name Person Handling Recall/Withdrawal: (at your facility)	

Date Notified:	Notification Method: (Email, Phone, etc.)	Product Description:	Product Identifier or Product Code:	Quantity on Hand: (incl. cases or eaches)

Was illness reported at your facility?	
Resolution: (Product destroyed, returned, etc.)	
Name Person Handling Recall/Withdrawal: (at your facility)	

Date Notified:	Notification Method: (Email, Phone, etc.)	Product Description:	Product Identifier or Product Code:	Quantity on Hand: (incl. cases or eaches)

Was illness reported at your facility?	
Resolution: (Product destroyed, returned, etc.)	
Name Person Handling Recall/Withdrawal: (at your facility)	

Date Notified:	Notification Method: (Email, Phone, etc.)	Product Description:	Product Identifier or Product Code:	Quantity on Hand: (incl. cases or eaches)
Was illness reported at your facility?				
Resolution: (Product destroyed, returned, etc.)				
Name Person Handling Recall/Withdrawal: (at your facility)				

Date Notified:	Notification Method: (Email, Phone, etc.)	Product Description:	Product Identifier or Product Code:	Quantity on Hand: (incl. cases or eaches)
Was illness reported at your facility?				
Resolution: (Product destroyed, returned, etc.)				
Name Person Handling Recall/Withdrawal: (at your facility)				

Date Notified:	Notification Method: (Email, Phone, etc.)	Product Description:	Product Identifier or Product Code:	Quantity on Hand: (incl. cases or eaches)
Was illness reported at your facility?				
Resolution: (Product destroyed, returned, etc.)				
Name Person Handling Recall/Withdrawal: (at your facility)				

Date Notified:	Notification Method: (Email, Phone, etc.)	Product Description:	Product Identifier or Product Code:	Quantity on Hand: (incl. cases or eaches)

Was illness reported at your facility?	
Resolution: (Product destroyed, returned, etc.)	
Name Person Handling Recall/Withdrawal: (at your facility)	

Date Notified:	Notification Method: (Email, Phone, etc.)	Product Description:	Product Identifier or Product Code:	Quantity on Hand: (incl. cases or eaches)

Was illness reported at your facility?	
Resolution: (Product destroyed, returned, etc.)	
Name Person Handling Recall/Withdrawal: (at your facility)	

Date Notified:	Notification Method: (Email, Phone, etc.)	Product Description:	Product Identifier or Product Code:	Quantity on Hand: (incl. cases or eaches)

Was illness reported at your facility?	
Resolution: (Product destroyed, returned, etc.)	
Name Person Handling Recall/Withdrawal: (at your facility)	

Date Notified:	Notification Method: (Email, Phone, etc.)	Product Description:	Product Identifier or Product Code:	Quantity on Hand: (incl. cases or eaches)

Was illness reported at your facility?	
Resolution: (Product destroyed, returned, etc.)	
Name Person Handling Recall/Withdrawal: (at your facility)	

Date Notified:	Notification Method: (Email, Phone, etc.)	Product Description:	Product Identifier or Product Code:	Quantity on Hand: (incl. cases or eaches)

Was illness reported at your facility?	
Resolution: (Product destroyed, returned, etc.)	
Name Person Handling Recall/Withdrawal: (at your facility)	

Date Notified:	Notification Method: (Email, Phone, etc.)	Product Description:	Product Identifier or Product Code:	Quantity on Hand: (incl. cases or eaches)

Was illness reported at your facility?	
Resolution: (Product destroyed, returned, etc.)	
Name Person Handling Recall/Withdrawal: (at your facility)	

Date Notified:	Notification Method: (Email, Phone, etc.)	Product Description:	Product Identifier or Product Code:	Quantity on Hand: (incl. cases or eaches)
Was illness reported at your facility?				
Resolution: (Product destroyed, returned, etc.)				
Name Person Handling Recall/Withdrawal: (at your facility)				

Date Notified:	Notification Method: (Email, Phone, etc.)	Product Description:	Product Identifier or Product Code:	Quantity on Hand: (incl. cases or eaches)
Was illness reported at your facility?				
Resolution: (Product destroyed, returned, etc.)				
Name Person Handling Recall/Withdrawal: (at your facility)				

Date Notified:	Notification Method: (Email, Phone, etc.)	Product Description:	Product Identifier or Product Code:	Quantity on Hand: (incl. cases or eaches)
Was illness reported at your facility?				
Resolution: (Product destroyed, returned, etc.)				
Name Person Handling Recall/Withdrawal: (at your facility)				

Date Notified:	Notification Method: (Email, Phone, etc.)	Product Description:	Product Identifier or Product Code:	Quantity on Hand: (incl. cases or eaches)

Was illness reported at your facility?	
Resolution: (Product destroyed, returned, etc.)	
Name Person Handling Recall/Withdrawal: (at your facility)	

Date Notified:	Notification Method: (Email, Phone, etc.)	Product Description:	Product Identifier or Product Code:	Quantity on Hand: (incl. cases or eaches)

Was illness reported at your facility?	
Resolution: (Product destroyed, returned, etc.)	
Name Person Handling Recall/Withdrawal: (at your facility)	

Date Notified:	Notification Method: (Email, Phone, etc.)	Product Description:	Product Identifier or Product Code:	Quantity on Hand: (incl. cases or eaches)

Was illness reported at your facility?	
Resolution: (Product destroyed, returned, etc.)	
Name Person Handling Recall/Withdrawal: (at your facility)	

Date Notified:	Notification Method: (Email, Phone, etc.)	Product Description:	Product Identifier or Product Code:	Quantity on Hand: (incl. cases or eaches)

Was illness reported at your facility?	
Resolution: (Product destroyed, returned, etc.)	
Name Person Handling Recall/Withdrawal: (at your facility)	

Date Notified:	Notification Method: (Email, Phone, etc.)	Product Description:	Product Identifier or Product Code:	Quantity on Hand: (incl. cases or eaches)

Was illness reported at your facility?	
Resolution: (Product destroyed, returned, etc.)	
Name Person Handling Recall/Withdrawal: (at your facility)	

Date Notified:	Notification Method: (Email, Phone, etc.)	Product Description:	Product Identifier or Product Code:	Quantity on Hand: (incl. cases or eaches)

Was illness reported at your facility?	
Resolution: (Product destroyed, returned, etc.)	
Name Person Handling Recall/Withdrawal: (at your facility)	

Date Notified:	Notification Method: (Email, Phone, etc.)	Product Description:	Product Identifier or Product Code:	Quantity on Hand: (incl. cases or eaches)

Was illness reported at your facility?	
Resolution: (Product destroyed, returned, etc.)	
Name Person Handling Recall/Withdrawal: (at your facility)	

Date Notified:	Notification Method: (Email, Phone, etc.)	Product Description:	Product Identifier or Product Code:	Quantity on Hand: (incl. cases or eaches)

Was illness reported at your facility?	
Resolution: (Product destroyed, returned, etc.)	
Name Person Handling Recall/Withdrawal: (at your facility)	

Date Notified:	Notification Method: (Email, Phone, etc.)	Product Description:	Product Identifier or Product Code:	Quantity on Hand: (incl. cases or eaches)

Was illness reported at your facility?	
Resolution: (Product destroyed, returned, etc.)	
Name Person Handling Recall/Withdrawal: (at your facility)	

Date Notified:	Notification Method: (Email, Phone, etc.)	Product Description:	Product Identifier or Product Code:	Quantity on Hand: (incl. cases or eaches)

Was illness reported at your facility?	
Resolution: (Product destroyed, returned, etc.)	
Name Person Handling Recall/Withdrawal: (at your facility)	

Date Notified:	Notification Method: (Email, Phone, etc.)	Product Description:	Product Identifier or Product Code:	Quantity on Hand: (incl. cases or eaches)

Was illness reported at your facility?	
Resolution: (Product destroyed, returned, etc.)	
Name Person Handling Recall/Withdrawal: (at your facility)	

Date Notified:	Notification Method: (Email, Phone, etc.)	Product Description:	Product Identifier or Product Code:	Quantity on Hand: (incl. cases or eaches)

Was illness reported at your facility?	
Resolution: (Product destroyed, returned, etc.)	
Name Person Handling Recall/Withdrawal: (at your facility)	

Date Notified:	Notification Method: (Email, Phone, etc.)	Product Description:	Product Identifier or Product Code:	Quantity on Hand: (incl. cases or eaches)
Was illness reported at your facility?				
Resolution: (Product destroyed, returned, etc.)				
Name Person Handling Recall/Withdrawal: (at your facility)				

Date Notified:	Notification Method: (Email, Phone, etc.)	Product Description:	Product Identifier or Product Code:	Quantity on Hand: (incl. cases or eaches)
Was illness reported at your facility?				
Resolution: (Product destroyed, returned, etc.)				
Name Person Handling Recall/Withdrawal: (at your facility)				

Date Notified:	Notification Method: (Email, Phone, etc.)	Product Description:	Product Identifier or Product Code:	Quantity on Hand: (incl. cases or eaches)
Was illness reported at your facility?				
Resolution: (Product destroyed, returned, etc.)				
Name Person Handling Recall/Withdrawal: (at your facility)				

Date Notified:	Notification Method: (Email, Phone, etc.)	Product Description:	Product Identifier or Product Code:	Quantity on Hand: (incl. cases or eaches)

Was illness reported at your facility?	
Resolution: (Product destroyed, returned, etc.)	
Name Person Handling Recall/Withdrawal: (at your facility)	

Date Notified:	Notification Method: (Email, Phone, etc.)	Product Description:	Product Identifier or Product Code:	Quantity on Hand: (incl. cases or eaches)

Was illness reported at your facility?	
Resolution: (Product destroyed, returned, etc.)	
Name Person Handling Recall/Withdrawal: (at your facility)	

Date Notified:	Notification Method: (Email, Phone, etc.)	Product Description:	Product Identifier or Product Code:	Quantity on Hand: (incl. cases or eaches)

Was illness reported at your facility?	
Resolution: (Product destroyed, returned, etc.)	
Name Person Handling Recall/Withdrawal: (at your facility)	

Date Notified:	Notification Method: (Email, Phone, etc.)	Product Description:	Product Identifier or Product Code:	Quantity on Hand: (incl. cases or eaches)
Was illness reported at your facility?				
Resolution: (Product destroyed, returned, etc.)				
Name Person Handling Recall/Withdrawal: (at your facility)				

Date Notified:	Notification Method: (Email, Phone, etc.)	Product Description:	Product Identifier or Product Code:	Quantity on Hand: (incl. cases or eaches)
Was illness reported at your facility?				
Resolution: (Product destroyed, returned, etc.)				
Name Person Handling Recall/Withdrawal: (at your facility)				

Date Notified:	Notification Method: (Email, Phone, etc.)	Product Description:	Product Identifier or Product Code:	Quantity on Hand: (incl. cases or eaches)
Was illness reported at your facility?				
Resolution: (Product destroyed, returned, etc.)				
Name Person Handling Recall/Withdrawal: (at your facility)				

Date Notified:	Notification Method: (Email, Phone, etc.)	Product Description:	Product Identifier or Product Code:	Quantity on Hand: (incl. cases or eaches)
Was illness reported at your facility?				
Resolution: (Product destroyed, returned, etc.)				
Name Person Handling Recall/Withdrawal: (at your facility)				

Date Notified:	Notification Method: (Email, Phone, etc.)	Product Description:	Product Identifier or Product Code:	Quantity on Hand: (incl. cases or eaches)
Was illness reported at your facility?				
Resolution: (Product destroyed, returned, etc.)				
Name Person Handling Recall/Withdrawal: (at your facility)				

Date Notified:	Notification Method: (Email, Phone, etc.)	Product Description:	Product Identifier or Product Code:	Quantity on Hand: (incl. cases or eaches)
Was illness reported at your facility?				
Resolution: (Product destroyed, returned, etc.)				
Name Person Handling Recall/Withdrawal: (at your facility)				

Date Notified:	Notification Method: (Email, Phone, etc.)	Product Description:	Product Identifier or Product Code:	Quantity on Hand: (incl. cases or eaches)

Was illness reported at your facility?	
Resolution: (Product destroyed, returned, etc.)	
Name Person Handling Recall/Withdrawal: (at your facility)	

Date Notified:	Notification Method: (Email, Phone, etc.)	Product Description:	Product Identifier or Product Code:	Quantity on Hand: (incl. cases or eaches)

Was illness reported at your facility?	
Resolution: (Product destroyed, returned, etc.)	
Name Person Handling Recall/Withdrawal: (at your facility)	

Date Notified:	Notification Method: (Email, Phone, etc.)	Product Description:	Product Identifier or Product Code:	Quantity on Hand: (incl. cases or eaches)

Was illness reported at your facility?	
Resolution: (Product destroyed, returned, etc.)	
Name Person Handling Recall/Withdrawal: (at your facility)	

Date Notified:	Notification Method: (Email, Phone, etc.)	Product Description:	Product Identifier or Product Code:	Quantity on Hand: (incl. cases or eaches)

Was illness reported at your facility?	
Resolution: (Product destroyed, returned, etc.)	
Name Person Handling Recall/Withdrawal: (at your facility)	

Date Notified:	Notification Method: (Email, Phone, etc.)	Product Description:	Product Identifier or Product Code:	Quantity on Hand: (incl. cases or eaches)

Was illness reported at your facility?	
Resolution: (Product destroyed, returned, etc.)	
Name Person Handling Recall/Withdrawal: (at your facility)	

Date Notified:	Notification Method: (Email, Phone, etc.)	Product Description:	Product Identifier or Product Code:	Quantity on Hand: (incl. cases or eaches)

Was illness reported at your facility?	
Resolution: (Product destroyed, returned, etc.)	
Name Person Handling Recall/Withdrawal: (at your facility)	

Date Notified:	Notification Method: (Email, Phone, etc.)	Product Description:	Product Identifier or Product Code:	Quantity on Hand: (incl. cases or eaches)

Was illness reported at your facility?	
Resolution: (Product destroyed, returned, etc.)	
Name Person Handling Recall/Withdrawal: (at your facility)	

Date Notified:	Notification Method: (Email, Phone, etc.)	Product Description:	Product Identifier or Product Code:	Quantity on Hand: (incl. cases or eaches)

Was illness reported at your facility?	
Resolution: (Product destroyed, returned, etc.)	
Name Person Handling Recall/Withdrawal: (at your facility)	

Date Notified:	Notification Method: (Email, Phone, etc.)	Product Description:	Product Identifier or Product Code:	Quantity on Hand: (incl. cases or eaches)

Was illness reported at your facility?	
Resolution: (Product destroyed, returned, etc.)	
Name Person Handling Recall/Withdrawal: (at your facility)	

Date Notified:	Notification Method: (Email, Phone, etc.)	Product Description:	Product Identifier or Product Code:	Quantity on Hand: (incl. cases or eaches)
Was illness reported at your facility?				
Resolution: (Product destroyed, returned, etc.)				
Name Person Handling Recall/Withdrawal: (at your facility)				

Date Notified:	Notification Method: (Email, Phone, etc.)	Product Description:	Product Identifier or Product Code:	Quantity on Hand: (incl. cases or eaches)
Was illness reported at your facility?				
Resolution: (Product destroyed, returned, etc.)				
Name Person Handling Recall/Withdrawal: (at your facility)				

Date Notified:	Notification Method: (Email, Phone, etc.)	Product Description:	Product Identifier or Product Code:	Quantity on Hand: (incl. cases or eaches)
Was illness reported at your facility?				
Resolution: (Product destroyed, returned, etc.)				
Name Person Handling Recall/Withdrawal: (at your facility)				

Date Notified:	Notification Method: (Email, Phone, etc.)	Product Description:	Product Identifier or Product Code:	Quantity on Hand: (incl. cases or eaches)

Was illness reported at your facility?	
Resolution: (Product destroyed, returned, etc.)	
Name Person Handling Recall/Withdrawal: (at your facility)	

Date Notified:	Notification Method: (Email, Phone, etc.)	Product Description:	Product Identifier or Product Code:	Quantity on Hand: (incl. cases or eaches)

Was illness reported at your facility?	
Resolution: (Product destroyed, returned, etc.)	
Name Person Handling Recall/Withdrawal: (at your facility)	

Date Notified:	Notification Method: (Email, Phone, etc.)	Product Description:	Product Identifier or Product Code:	Quantity on Hand: (incl. cases or eaches)

Was illness reported at your facility?	
Resolution: (Product destroyed, returned, etc.)	
Name Person Handling Recall/Withdrawal: (at your facility)	

Date Notified:	Notification Method: (Email, Phone, etc.)	Product Description:	Product Identifier or Product Code:	Quantity on Hand: (incl. cases or eaches)
Was illness reported at your facility?			
Resolution: (Product destroyed, returned, etc.)			
Name Person Handling Recall/Withdrawal: (at your facility)			

Date Notified:	Notification Method: (Email, Phone, etc.)	Product Description:	Product Identifier or Product Code:	Quantity on Hand: (incl. cases or eaches)
Was illness reported at your facility?			
Resolution: (Product destroyed, returned, etc.)			
Name Person Handling Recall/Withdrawal: (at your facility)			

Date Notified:	Notification Method: (Email, Phone, etc.)	Product Description:	Product Identifier or Product Code:	Quantity on Hand: (incl. cases or eaches)
Was illness reported at your facility?			
Resolution: (Product destroyed, returned, etc.)			
Name Person Handling Recall/Withdrawal: (at your facility)			

Date Notified:	Notification Method: (Email, Phone, etc.)	Product Description:	Product Identifier or Product Code:	Quantity on Hand: (incl. cases or eaches)

Was illness reported at your facility?	
Resolution: (Product destroyed, returned, etc.)	
Name Person Handling Recall/Withdrawal: (at your facility)	

Date Notified:	Notification Method: (Email, Phone, etc.)	Product Description:	Product Identifier or Product Code:	Quantity on Hand: (incl. cases or eaches)

Was illness reported at your facility?	
Resolution: (Product destroyed, returned, etc.)	
Name Person Handling Recall/Withdrawal: (at your facility)	

Date Notified:	Notification Method: (Email, Phone, etc.)	Product Description:	Product Identifier or Product Code:	Quantity on Hand: (incl. cases or eaches)

Was illness reported at your facility?	
Resolution: (Product destroyed, returned, etc.)	
Name Person Handling Recall/Withdrawal: (at your facility)	

Date Notified:	Notification Method: (Email, Phone, etc.)	Product Description:	Product Identifier or Product Code:	Quantity on Hand: (incl. cases or eaches)

Was illness reported at your facility?	
Resolution: (Product destroyed, returned, etc.)	
Name Person Handling Recall/Withdrawal: (at your facility)	

Date Notified:	Notification Method: (Email, Phone, etc.)	Product Description:	Product Identifier or Product Code:	Quantity on Hand: (incl. cases or eaches)

Was illness reported at your facility?	
Resolution: (Product destroyed, returned, etc.)	
Name Person Handling Recall/Withdrawal: (at your facility)	

Date Notified:	Notification Method: (Email, Phone, etc.)	Product Description:	Product Identifier or Product Code:	Quantity on Hand: (incl. cases or eaches)

Was illness reported at your facility?	
Resolution: (Product destroyed, returned, etc.)	
Name Person Handling Recall/Withdrawal: (at your facility)	

Date Notified:	Notification Method: (Email, Phone, etc.)	Product Description:	Product Identifier or Product Code:	Quantity on Hand: (incl. cases or eaches)
Was illness reported at your facility?				
Resolution: (Product destroyed, returned, etc.)				
Name Person Handling Recall/Withdrawal: (at your facility)				

Date Notified:	Notification Method: (Email, Phone, etc.)	Product Description:	Product Identifier or Product Code:	Quantity on Hand: (incl. cases or eaches)
Was illness reported at your facility?				
Resolution: (Product destroyed, returned, etc.)				
Name Person Handling Recall/Withdrawal: (at your facility)				

Date Notified:	Notification Method: (Email, Phone, etc.)	Product Description:	Product Identifier or Product Code:	Quantity on Hand: (incl. cases or eaches)
Was illness reported at your facility?				
Resolution: (Product destroyed, returned, etc.)				
Name Person Handling Recall/Withdrawal: (at your facility)				

Date Notified:	Notification Method: (Email, Phone, etc.)	Product Description:	Product Identifier or Product Code:	Quantity on Hand: (incl. cases or eaches)

Was illness reported at your facility?	
Resolution: (Product destroyed, returned, etc.)	
Name Person Handling Recall/Withdrawal: (at your facility)	

Date Notified:	Notification Method: (Email, Phone, etc.)	Product Description:	Product Identifier or Product Code:	Quantity on Hand: (incl. cases or eaches)

Was illness reported at your facility?	
Resolution: (Product destroyed, returned, etc.)	
Name Person Handling Recall/Withdrawal: (at your facility)	

Date Notified:	Notification Method: (Email, Phone, etc.)	Product Description:	Product Identifier or Product Code:	Quantity on Hand: (incl. cases or eaches)

Was illness reported at your facility?	
Resolution: (Product destroyed, returned, etc.)	
Name Person Handling Recall/Withdrawal: (at your facility)	

Date Notified:	Notification Method: (Email, Phone, etc.)	Product Description:	Product Identifier or Product Code:	Quantity on Hand: (incl. cases or eaches)

Was illness reported at your facility?	
Resolution: (Product destroyed, returned, etc.)	
Name Person Handling Recall/Withdrawal: (at your facility)	

Date Notified:	Notification Method: (Email, Phone, etc.)	Product Description:	Product Identifier or Product Code:	Quantity on Hand: (incl. cases or eaches)

Was illness reported at your facility?	
Resolution: (Product destroyed, returned, etc.)	
Name Person Handling Recall/Withdrawal: (at your facility)	

Date Notified:	Notification Method: (Email, Phone, etc.)	Product Description:	Product Identifier or Product Code:	Quantity on Hand: (incl. cases or eaches)

Was illness reported at your facility?	
Resolution: (Product destroyed, returned, etc.)	
Name Person Handling Recall/Withdrawal: (at your facility)	

Date Notified:	Notification Method: (Email, Phone, etc.)	Product Description:	Product Identifier or Product Code:	Quantity on Hand: (incl. cases or eaches)

Was illness reported at your facility?	
Resolution: (Product destroyed, returned, etc.)	
Name Person Handling Recall/Withdrawal: (at your facility)	

Date Notified:	Notification Method: (Email, Phone, etc.)	Product Description:	Product Identifier or Product Code:	Quantity on Hand: (incl. cases or eaches)

Was illness reported at your facility?	
Resolution: (Product destroyed, returned, etc.)	
Name Person Handling Recall/Withdrawal: (at your facility)	

Date Notified:	Notification Method: (Email, Phone, etc.)	Product Description:	Product Identifier or Product Code:	Quantity on Hand: (incl. cases or eaches)

Was illness reported at your facility?	
Resolution: (Product destroyed, returned, etc.)	
Name Person Handling Recall/Withdrawal: (at your facility)	

Date Notified:	Notification Method: (Email, Phone, etc.)	Product Description:	Product Identifier or Product Code:	Quantity on Hand: (incl. cases or eaches)

Was illness reported at your facility?	
Resolution: (Product destroyed, returned, etc.)	
Name Person Handling Recall/Withdrawal: (at your facility)	

Date Notified:	Notification Method: (Email, Phone, etc.)	Product Description:	Product Identifier or Product Code:	Quantity on Hand: (incl. cases or eaches)

Was illness reported at your facility?	
Resolution: (Product destroyed, returned, etc.)	
Name Person Handling Recall/Withdrawal: (at your facility)	

Date Notified:	Notification Method: (Email, Phone, etc.)	Product Description:	Product Identifier or Product Code:	Quantity on Hand: (incl. cases or eaches)

Was illness reported at your facility?	
Resolution: (Product destroyed, returned, etc.)	
Name Person Handling Recall/Withdrawal: (at your facility)	

Date Notified:	Notification Method: (Email, Phone, etc.)	Product Description:	Product Identifier or Product Code:	Quantity on Hand: (incl. cases or eaches)

Was illness reported at your facility?	
Resolution: (Product destroyed, returned, etc.)	
Name Person Handling Recall/Withdrawal: (at your facility)	

Date Notified:	Notification Method: (Email, Phone, etc.)	Product Description:	Product Identifier or Product Code:	Quantity on Hand: (incl. cases or eaches)

Was illness reported at your facility?	
Resolution: (Product destroyed, returned, etc.)	
Name Person Handling Recall/Withdrawal: (at your facility)	

Date Notified:	Notification Method: (Email, Phone, etc.)	Product Description:	Product Identifier or Product Code:	Quantity on Hand: (incl. cases or eaches)

Was illness reported at your facility?	
Resolution: (Product destroyed, returned, etc.)	
Name Person Handling Recall/Withdrawal: (at your facility)	

Date Notified:	Notification Method: (Email, Phone, etc.)	Product Description:	Product Identifier or Product Code:	Quantity on Hand: (incl. cases or eaches)

Was illness reported at your facility?	
Resolution: (Product destroyed, returned, etc.)	
Name Person Handling Recall/Withdrawal: (at your facility)	

Date Notified:	Notification Method: (Email, Phone, etc.)	Product Description:	Product Identifier or Product Code:	Quantity on Hand: (incl. cases or eaches)

Was illness reported at your facility?	
Resolution: (Product destroyed, returned, etc.)	
Name Person Handling Recall/Withdrawal: (at your facility)	

Date Notified:	Notification Method: (Email, Phone, etc.)	Product Description:	Product Identifier or Product Code:	Quantity on Hand: (incl. cases or eaches)

Was illness reported at your facility?	
Resolution: (Product destroyed, returned, etc.)	
Name Person Handling Recall/Withdrawal: (at your facility)	

Date Notified:	Notification Method: (Email, Phone, etc.)	Product Description:	Product Identifier or Product Code:	Quantity on Hand: (incl. cases or eaches)
Was illness reported at your facility?				
Resolution: (Product destroyed, returned, etc.)				
Name Person Handling Recall/Withdrawal: (at your facility)				

Date Notified:	Notification Method: (Email, Phone, etc.)	Product Description:	Product Identifier or Product Code:	Quantity on Hand: (incl. cases or eaches)
Was illness reported at your facility?				
Resolution: (Product destroyed, returned, etc.)				
Name Person Handling Recall/Withdrawal: (at your facility)				

Date Notified:	Notification Method: (Email, Phone, etc.)	Product Description:	Product Identifier or Product Code:	Quantity on Hand: (incl. cases or eaches)
Was illness reported at your facility?				
Resolution: (Product destroyed, returned, etc.)				
Name Person Handling Recall/Withdrawal: (at your facility)				

Date Notified:	Notification Method: (Email, Phone, etc.)	Product Description:	Product Identifier or Product Code:	Quantity on Hand: (incl. cases or eaches)

Was illness reported at your facility?	
Resolution: (Product destroyed, returned, etc.)	
Name Person Handling Recall/Withdrawal: (at your facility)	

Date Notified:	Notification Method: (Email, Phone, etc.)	Product Description:	Product Identifier or Product Code:	Quantity on Hand: (incl. cases or eaches)

Was illness reported at your facility?	
Resolution: (Product destroyed, returned, etc.)	
Name Person Handling Recall/Withdrawal: (at your facility)	

Date Notified:	Notification Method: (Email, Phone, etc.)	Product Description:	Product Identifier or Product Code:	Quantity on Hand: (incl. cases or eaches)

Was illness reported at your facility?	
Resolution: (Product destroyed, returned, etc.)	
Name Person Handling Recall/Withdrawal: (at your facility)	

Date Notified:	Notification Method: (Email, Phone, etc.)	Product Description:	Product Identifier or Product Code:	Quantity on Hand: (incl. cases or eaches)
Was illness reported at your facility?				
Resolution: (Product destroyed, returned, etc.)				
Name Person Handling Recall/Withdrawal: (at your facility)				

Date Notified:	Notification Method: (Email, Phone, etc.)	Product Description:	Product Identifier or Product Code:	Quantity on Hand: (incl. cases or eaches)
Was illness reported at your facility?				
Resolution: (Product destroyed, returned, etc.)				
Name Person Handling Recall/Withdrawal: (at your facility)				

Date Notified:	Notification Method: (Email, Phone, etc.)	Product Description:	Product Identifier or Product Code:	Quantity on Hand: (incl. cases or eaches)
Was illness reported at your facility?				
Resolution: (Product destroyed, returned, etc.)				
Name Person Handling Recall/Withdrawal: (at your facility)				

Date Notified:	Notification Method: (Email, Phone, etc.)	Product Description:	Product Identifier or Product Code:	Quantity on Hand: (incl. cases or eaches)

Was illness reported at your facility?	
Resolution: (Product destroyed, returned, etc.)	
Name Person Handling Recall/Withdrawal: (at your facility)	

Date Notified:	Notification Method: (Email, Phone, etc.)	Product Description:	Product Identifier or Product Code:	Quantity on Hand: (incl. cases or eaches)

Was illness reported at your facility?	
Resolution: (Product destroyed, returned, etc.)	
Name Person Handling Recall/Withdrawal: (at your facility)	

Date Notified:	Notification Method: (Email, Phone, etc.)	Product Description:	Product Identifier or Product Code:	Quantity on Hand: (incl. cases or eaches)

Was illness reported at your facility?	
Resolution: (Product destroyed, returned, etc.)	
Name Person Handling Recall/Withdrawal: (at your facility)	

www.ingramcontent.com/pod-product-compliance
Lightning Source LLC
Chambersburg PA
CBHW080537190526
45169CB00007B/2528